The Plastic Plague

Written by Joshua Hatch

Flying Start
to Literacy®

Contents

Chapter 4
What is the future of plastic? 20

Introduction

Plastic is an amazing material. It can be made into almost any shape, and it can be made into any colour. Or it can be clear so that you can see through it!

If you look around, you'll see plastic everywhere.

More and more people are worried that we use too much plastic. When we no longer need it, we throw it away, and most of it ends up in rivers, lakes and oceans. This is harmful to the animals that live there.

Can we keep using plastic without damaging our environment? That's the challenge!

Chapter 1

What is plastic?

Most plastics are made from oil and natural gas – the same kind of fuels used to power our cars and heat our homes. Different ways of **processing** the oil and gas make different kinds of plastic.

Some plastics are soft, while others are hard. Some plastics are stiff, and others can bend and are **flexible**. One example of light and flexible plastic is plastic food wrap. Other plastics are strong and stiff, like the plastic used to make cups.

Did you know?

The word *plastic* comes from ancient Greek. It means mouldable, in the same way clay or bubblegum can be shaped and reshaped.

Why is plastic everywhere?

Plastic is light in weight, and it can last for a very long time without wearing out or breaking. No wonder we use so much of it.

Light in weight

Something made from plastic usually weighs less than the same thing made from glass or metal. Things that weigh less cost less to transport from a factory to a shop, or from city to city, or from one country to another. So, making packaging out of lightweight plastic, instead of heavy glass or metal, saves money.

Lasts for a long time

Things made from plastic last longer. Plastic jars don't break very easily, and it's difficult to tear most plastic wrappers.

But this is part of the problem. When plastic things are thrown away, they don't break down. They stay the way they are for hundreds of years.

Plastic wonder

Can you find at least five different things in your home made from plastic?

Chapter 2

Plastic or natural materials – which is better?

Everything around you is made from some **material**. The paper in this book is made from wood pulp. Windows are made from glass, and glass is made from sand. Part of your shoes, might be made from leather. These materials are natural. Over time, they will naturally break down. They often look better and feel better than plastic.

But sometimes, **natural materials** don't work very well. Glass jars shatter. Paper rips. Metal rusts. Many of these materials are also heavy and can be difficult or expensive to make.

Did you know?

In the past, ivory was used to make many things, including jewellery and white piano keys. But ivory comes from elephant tusks. To get the ivory, elephants must be killed.

Each year, about 27,000 elephants are killed for their tusks. If this continues, there will be no more elephants by the year 2040. Using plastic, instead of ivory, helps save elephants.

Is plastic really better?

In some ways, plastic is an improvement over natural materials. A metal toy can dent or rust, and wooden toys can splinter or the paint can peel.

Plastic doesn't shatter like glass or splinter like wood. And many plastic toys can bend back into shape.

One of the most important things about plastic is that it usually costs less than natural materials. It's cheaper and faster to make a plastic bowl than a glass bowl.

But natural materials have their benefits, too. If cared for, natural materials can be used for much longer than plastic materials. It's also easier to repair an object made from metal or wood than one made from plastic.

Natural materials are also easier to reuse or recycle. Glass and metal can be melted to make new jars and cans, but that's harder to do with plastic.

Chapter 3

What is the problem with plastic?

Lots of plastic, such as plastic bags and plastic wrap, is used only once and then it's thrown away – it's **disposable**. We now have a huge amount of plastic rubbish, and, as we know, plastic lasts a long time. This is the problem.

What happens to plastic rubbish?

Each year, every person in the United States, Europe and Australia throws away between 10 and 90 kilograms of plastic. Most plastic rubbish ends up in **landfills** or in the environment. Only a small amount is recycled.

Plastic does not **decompose** – it does not rot away like wood, paper or cotton. Instead, it breaks apart into smaller and smaller pieces of plastic that build up in our environment.

Did you know?

It takes about 450 years for a plastic water bottle to break down.

The Great Pacific Garbage Patch

In the Pacific Ocean, there is a huge patch of garbage called the Great Pacific Garbage Patch. It is made up of tiny pieces of rubbish – mostly plastic – and it floats over an area of at least 1.6 million square kilometres. That's roughly the size of the state of Queensland!

Sometimes, animals will eat small pieces of this plastic and it makes them sick.

Seawater with tiny pieces of plastic rubbish

We are putting so much plastic in the ocean that experts say by 2050 there will be more plastic in the water than there are fish.

Did you know?

In the past 70 years, we have produced about eight billion tonnes of plastic, and thrown away about six billion tonnes. The plastic we have thrown away weighs about the same as one billion elephants!

How does plastic get in the ocean?

Almost half of the plastic made is used just for packaging and then is thrown away.

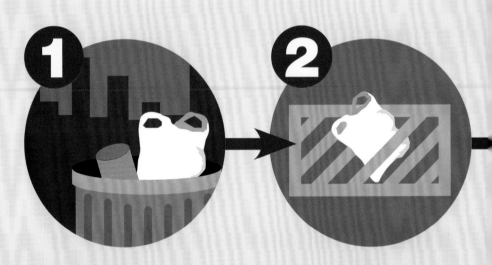

Plastic bag from a shop in the city blows from a rubbish bin . . .

into a storm drain. It travels through pipes and waterways . . .

Plastic rubbish from rubbish bins, the streets and landfills makes its way into storm drains. Rubbish travels through sewer pipes, into waterways, and finally into the ocean.

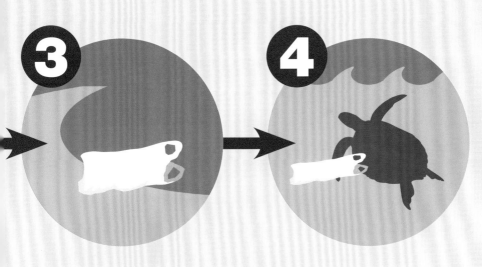

into the ocean . . .

where marine wildlife mistakes it for food.

Chapter 4

What is the future of plastic?

The biggest problem with plastic is what it does to the environment. To solve this problem, people are trying to do three things:

- make new plastics that **decompose** in the environment
- recycle more plastic
- use less plastic.

Did you know?

An adult fleece jacket can be made from about 25 recycled plastic water bottles.

Scientists are experimenting with biodegradable pots for plants.

Plastic that decomposes

The best solution is to make plastics that will decompose. To do this, scientists are working on making plastics from plants.

These new plastics will decompose just like food waste. Over time, they will turn into natural, **organic** materials instead of polluting our oceans. That would go a long way towards making plastics better for the environment.

Recycling

Recycling plastic is another way to help reduce plastic rubbish. Plastic cartons can be turned into jungle gyms. Plastic bags can be turned into park benches. And plastic foam can be turned into home **insulation**.

Most plastics have a symbol on them – a triangle with a number between one and seven. The number tells you what type of plastic the item is made from. Plastics with the same numbers can be recycled together.

Seven types of plastic

Most plastic items have a number to identify the type of plastic.

Symbol	Common forms	What it can be recycled into
1	soft-drink bottles, peanut butter and jelly jars	fibrefill for sleeping bags, carpet fibres, rope, pillows
2	milk and juice bottles, shampoo bottles, grocery bags	flowerpots, rubbish bins, traffic barrier cones, detergent bottles
3	trays for lollies and fruit, plastic wrap	drainage and irrigation pipes
4	grocery bags, bread bags, shrink-wrap, margarine tub tops	grocery bags, plastic lumber
5	furniture, luggage, bottle caps	plastic lumber, car battery cases, steps
6	toys, hot-drink cups, packaging materials (peanuts), meat trays	plastic lumber, plastic boxes, flowerpots
7	baby bottles, hard cups, water cooler bottles, car parts	These items can't be recycled because they are made from a mixture of plastics.

Use less plastic

Many plastic items that we use every day are used only once before they are thrown away or recycled. These items are called single-use plastics, and they include plastic bags, straws, water bottles and most food packaging.

To use less plastic, people are choosing items made from **natural materials**. Instead of plastic straws, people are using paper or reusable metal straws. Instead of plastic bags, people are bringing reusable cloth bags to the shops.

Many countries around the world are now banning single-use plastics.

Conclusion

Because plastic is such an amazing **material**, we want to keep using it. To do this, we must solve the problem of plastic.

Because we have lots of plastic rubbish that is harming the environment, scientists are working to make better plastics. They are trying to make plastics that can be easily recycled or that **decompose** naturally.

Glossary

decompose to break down into natural components

disposable something that is used either only once or a limited number of times and then thrown away

flexible something that can bend easily

insulation a material that is used to stop heat or sound from getting out

landfills large areas where rubbish is buried under the ground

material the substance used to make something

natural materials substances that come from plants or animals; they also include things such as metals that are naturally formed under the ground

organic made up of or from living things; something that is not made of artificial chemicals

processing a series of actions intended to create a result

Index